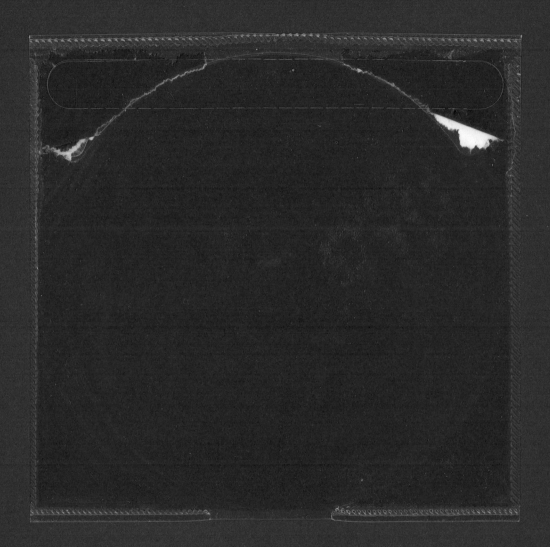

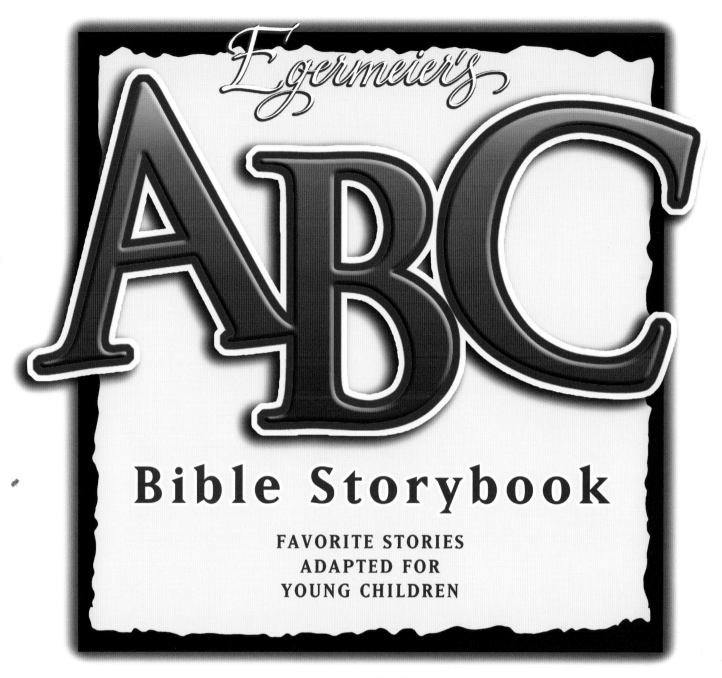

# Egermeier's
# ABC
# Bible Storybook

### FAVORITE STORIES
### ADAPTED FOR
### YOUNG CHILDREN

Favorite Stories by Elsie Egermeier
Adapted by Arlene Hall

Illustrations: Laura Nikiel
Layout: Curt Corzine
Editor: Karen Rhodes

 Warner Press

 WP Kids

# Adam & Eve

God made the first man and breathed life into his body. God called the first man Adam. God gave Adam the job of naming all creatures that had been created. Adam was to rule over all other living things. That was a big job! Adam needed a helper.

God said, "It is not good that man should be alone. I will make him a helper." So God made Adam a wife. Adam loved her very much. He called his wife Eve.

Adam and Eve were very happy in their garden home—the Garden of Eden. God gave them everything they needed to survive—the best fruits and vegetables to be found—soft grass and lots of beautiful trees and flowers. All that God gave them was good. Nothing in the garden was bad or evil. Nothing bad happened there.

Best of all, God met them in the garden every evening. He walked and talked with them every evening, and the weather was perfect.

Story from Genesis 1—2:24

# Baby Jesus

"We have to go to Bethlehem," Joseph told Mary. "We have to have our names put in the king's book. He has ordered it."

Soon the streets of Bethlehem were filled with travelers. By the time Joseph and Mary got there, no rooms were left anywhere. After they had searched for hours an innkeeper told Joseph, "I have a stable where you can stay." Mary and Joseph thanked the kind man.

That night a wonderful thing happened! Baby Jesus was born. Mary put him in clean, warm blankets and laid him in the manger that Joseph had filled with clean, sweet hay. Mary and Joseph were so thankful for their new son.

Joseph and Mary knew their baby was special. He was Jesus—sent from God. When he grew up he would tell people about God.

**Story from Luke 2:1-8**

# Creation

Long ago there was no world at all. There was no sun to shine, no stars to twinkle, no moonbeams to play through the night shadows.

But even then there was God. At the beginning of time God made the world. At first water covered everything and darkness was everywhere. It was a strange, unfriendly world but God planned to make it beautiful, so he said, "Let there be light." He called the light Day and the darkness Night.

For seven days God worked his plan of creation. He made the beautiful blue sky and placed in it clouds to carry moisture. God said, "Let the waters be gathered together into one place and let dry land appear." He called the waters Seas and the dry land Earth. He made trees and plants. God knew his work was good.

Then God made the sun, the moon and the stars—the sun to rule the day and the moon, the night. Next, God began creating fish to swim in the seas, birds to fly in the sky and all kinds of living creatures. But there were no people, no homes, no children. So God created Adam and Eve—people who would enjoy the earth and take care of it. They would be able to love and worship God. It took six days to create everything God had planned; then on the seventh day God rested.

**Story from Genesis 1:1—2:24**

# David the Shepherd Boy

Something was wrong with the king. He acted as if he were out of his mind! No one was able to help him. Would he ever be well again? King Saul was afraid.

The servants said "Let's send for young David. He can play soft music on his harp. His music will make you feel better. Then you'll be able to think clearly again."

David was brave, wise and good-looking. He took care of his father's sheep. In the long hours as he watched over them, he played on his harp. David made up songs of praise to God. Many of his songs (called Psalms) are in the Bible.

At the palace David played his harp for King Saul. His music quieted King Saul and made him feel better. Now he could think clearly again. No wonder he wanted David to stay on at the palace. The king was so thankful for David and his music.

Story from
1 Samuel 16:14-23

# Elisha's Caring Friends

Elisha walked from one town to another teaching people about God. He often grew tired and hungry. One day a very kind woman saw him and sent a servant to invite him to her house. Then she gave him food.

Elisha was happy to sit down and rest—his feet hurt. And he liked the good food. "Please come again," the woman told him. "Come rest and eat with us whenever you come to town." Elisha thanked her. After that Elisha stopped by often. He ate lunch with the kind woman and her husband.

One day the woman said to her husband, "Let's build a room for Elisha to use when he comes to town." The next time Elisha came he found a really nice room ready for him. It had a bed, a table and chair, and a lamp. Elisha was so thankful for these wonderful people who cared for him.

**Story from 2 Kings 4:8-11**

# Fishermen

One day while Peter and his brother were fishing near the shore, a man came walking by. He stopped for a while and watched them work.

When they got close to shore Peter and Andrew saw the man was Jesus. They had seen and heard Jesus speak before. They knew he was doing great things to help people. When they pulled their boat on shore Jesus talked about the work he wanted them to do.

Peter and Andrew were happy to leave their nets and boats to follow Jesus. Other fishermen followed Jesus too. Jesus loved his friends and taught them many things about God.

After working and spending lots of time with Jesus, these fishermen began to tell others about God's love. They traveled all over teaching people about God, just as Jesus had taught them to do. They brought happiness to many people.

**Story from Mark 1:16-17**

# Good Samaritan

One day a man asked Jesus, "Who is my neighbor?" To answer him Jesus told a story. A man was traveling from Jerusalem to Jericho. Along the way robbers beat him, stole his money, and left him to die.

Along came a priest but he did not stop to help. Then a Levite saw the man who was injured, lying by the road, but he quickly passed by.

Later a Samaritan came by. Quickly he got off his mule and helped the man. Then he took the stranger to an inn where he could have rest and food. The Samaritan gave the innkeeper money to care for the hurt man until he was well.

Then Jesus asked which man acted like a neighbor. "The good man from Samaria," answered the lawyer.

"Then if you would be a good neighbor, do as the Samaritan did," said Jesus.

**Story from Luke 10:24-37**

# Hosanna!

All the people of Jerusalem were excited. Crowds of them went out of the city gate and hurried down the road. Many of them had come to Jerusalem for the Passover. And they wanted to meet Jesus.

As Jesus and his disciples neared Jerusalem he said to two of them, "Go to the village nearby and get a colt for me." The disciples brought the colt to Jesus and put their coats on its back. Then Jesus sat on the colt. Many people put their clothes along the road for Jesus to ride over. Others waved palm branches. They shouted, "Blessed is the King who is coming in the name of the Lord! Peace in heaven and glory in the highest!"

As Jesus rode into the city and up to the temple, the people shouted, "Hosanna! Blessed is he that comes in the name of the Lord!"

Story from
Matthew 21:1-11

# Isle of Patmos

On a lonely island, far from his friends and home, sat an old man. When he was a young fisherman on the Sea of Galilee, he had left his nets to follow a dear friend, Jesus. The old man's name was John, one of the twelve disciples who followed Jesus for three years. Now John was a prisoner on this Isle of Patmos—a prisoner because he believed in Jesus.

John was thinking about God and remembered this was the day Christians met to worship. Then John heard a voice that sounded like the blast of a trumpet. The voice said, "I am Alpha and Omega, the first and the last. Write what you see in a book and send it to the seven churches of Asia."

John turned to see who was talking—he saw someone who looked like Jesus. But John had never seen his Master look like this! Jesus wore a long robe with a wide gold belt around his chest. In his right hand were seven stars and his face shone like the sun at noon. When he spoke his voice sounded like the rushing of mighty waters.

John fell as if dead at Jesus' feet, but Jesus bent over, touched John and said, "Do not be afraid. Write the things you see and hear." John heard and saw many things and he wrote them all down. We know this book today as the last book in the Bible—Revelation.

From the Book of Revelation

18

# Joseph

While Joseph's older brothers worked in the fields and cared for the animals, Joseph ran errands for his father, Jacob.

When Joseph was seventeen, his father said, "I have made you a coat of many colors because you bring me joy." Joseph loved his new coat and wore it often.

One day Jacob sent Joseph to the field where his brothers were working. The jealous brothers tore the coat off his back and put him into a deep hole in the ground. Then they sold Joseph to foreign travelers who took him to a land far away from his home.

Back home the brothers showed their father the coat. "We found this lying in the field," they said. Their father thought Joseph was dead.

But God took care of Joseph and helped him grow to be a great and good man in Egypt. Later his family came to live there too.

**Story from Genesis 37**

# King Solomon

When Solomon became king he took one thousand offerings to be burned on the altar to God. All day he prayed for God's help. When night came he lay down to sleep and had a wonderful dream. In the dream God asked Solomon, "What shall I give you?"

King Solomon answered quickly "I don't know how to be king. I rule over more people than I can count. Help me understand them so I'll be able to know the good from the bad. Help me to help my people."

God was happy that Solomon didn't ask for a lot of things for himself. God said, "You didn't ask for anything for yourself. I will give you a wise heart that makes good choices because it understands. No other person will be like you."

Because Solomon was so wise and intelligent God trusted him to build the temple. Solomon worked peacefully with other nations and their kings to build the Lord's temple. Solomon and his workers spent seven years building the Temple of the Lord.

## Story from 1 Kings 3, 5, 6

# Lions' Den and Daniel

Daniel was a man who loved and obeyed God. Because he loved God, Daniel prayed three times a day, even though the king made a law that people were to make requests only to him, not to their gods. Daniel did not hide or pray in secret where no one could hear him. He prayed in his house with the windows open so all would know he was praying to his God.

Men who hated Daniel complained to King Darius and reminded him of the law they had asked him to sign. The king was very upset! He didn't want to hurt Daniel, but he had no way out of punishing one who had broken the law. King Darius ordered guards to throw Daniel into a den with lions. The king was very upset and told Daniel, "The God you serve so faithfully will surely save you from the lions."

King Darius did not sleep, eat or listen to music all night long. When day came he hurried to the lions' den and called out, "O Daniel, servant of the living God, has your God saved you from the lions?"

From deep in the pit he heard Daniel answer, "O King, live forever. My God has sent his angel to shut the lions' mouths and they did not harm me. God knew I had done no wrong." King Darius was so happy. He had the guards pull Daniel out of the den and throw the men who had tried to harm Daniel in with the lions.

**Story from Daniel 6**

# Moses and the Red Sea

Moses and Aaron led the Israelites out of Egypt. In daylight God led the people by a great cloud. At night the cloud became a pillar of fire and he watched over them as they slept. By day or night the Israelites could look at the cloud or the pillar and say, "Our God is going with us, and he is leading the way."

God led them to the Red Sea where they planned to camp and rest from their long march. Suddenly someone ran through the camp shouting, "Pharaoh's army is coming! We'll be taken prisoners or killed!"

The Israelites could not swim across the Red Sea and they couldn't fight the army. They were so scared! At first they blamed Moses, "Why did you bring us out here in the wilderness to die? We would rather be slaves in Egypt than die here." But Moses wasn't to blame. When Moses cried to God for help, the Lord told Moses to speak to the people. He told them, "Fear not. Stand still and see the salvation of the Lord."

God told Moses, "Lift your rod over the Red Sea and divide it." Moses obeyed and God sent a strong wind that made a wide path and dried the ground. On each side of the path the waters rose like high walls until every one of the Israelites had crossed to the other side.

Pharaoh's army tried to follow the Israelites, but when they were far from shore the walls of water fell down and the whole army was drowned.

## Story from Exodus 13:20—15:21

# Noah and the Flood

Noah loved God and tried to do right. He taught his sons to do right also, and this pleased God. Sometimes God talked to Noah. God told Noah he was going to destroy the world that was bad and full of sinful people. God promised Noah and his family they would not be destroyed with the wicked people.

"Build an ark," God told Noah. "When it is finished you, your wife and your sons and their wives may go into the ark. Live there until the flood is over." God saved two of each kind of living thing. They would also stay in the ark during the flood.

Because Noah believed God he built the ark, just the way God told him. It looked like a three-story houseboat on dry land. People laughed at Noah. They thought he was crazy. Where was the water for the boat? Noah warned the people over and over to repent of their sins or die in the flood. But none believed him.

When all was ready and all were aboard, the rain began to fall—great sheets of it. The rain fell for forty days and nights. People realized Noah had been telling the truth, but it was too late. The water lifted the ark off the ground and it began to float. One day the ark landed on top of a mountain.

When the waters went away dry land appeared again. God told Noah he could open the ark's door and let everyone out. God put a rainbow in the sky to remind us of his promise that he would never again send a flood to destroy the earth.

**Story from Genesis 5:1—9:17**

# Onesimus Believes

Onesimus, a runaway slave, found a good friend in Paul. After hearing Paul tell about Jesus Onesimus became a Christian. For a time he took care of Paul in prison and learned more about Jesus.

Onesimus said, "I still belong to my master, Philemon. I will never feel right until I return to him."

To make sure Philemon would treat his runaway slave kindly, Paul wrote him: "Onesimus has been like a son to me while I am in prison. I wish he could have stayed on with me. Please take him back, not as a servant, but as a brother. Treat him as you would treat me. If he has wronged you or owes you anything charge it to me. I will repay it."

Then Onesimus took the letter and went on his way.

Story from the book of Philemon.

30

# Paul on the Road to Damascus

Paul believed in the Law of Moses. He thought Jesus and his followers were not respecting the Law, so Paul hated them. In fact, Paul had put many believers of Jesus in prison and had been mean to them.

Paul asked the high priest to write letters to rulers of the synagogues in Damascus—that they should help Paul find the believers in Damascus and kill them or put them in prison.

One day Paul and his friends were close to Damascus. Suddenly they stopped as a great, bright light from heaven shone on Paul, blinding him. As Paul fell to the ground a voice from heaven called, "Why are you persecuting me?"

Paul was amazed and terrified. He thought he was protecting the true religion when he opposed those who believed in Jesus. He cried out, "Who are you, Lord?"

A voice answered, "I am Jesus of Nazareth whom you are fighting against. It is hard for you to oppose me."

Paul was led into Damascus where he sat in darkness. He was not able to eat or drink because he realized he had been wrong. God sent a man to see Paul. Ananias said, "The Lord Jesus, who appeared to you on the road, has sent me so you would receive your sight and be filled with the Holy Spirit."

From that day forward Paul preached that Christ is the Son of God.

**Story from Acts 9:1-19**

# Quail for Whining People

The Israelites were resting in their tents, some whining over their hard life. God heard and was angry. Fire fell on part of the camp and some died. The people were afraid and cried to Moses for help. He prayed and God put out the fire.

The Israelites traveled until they came to another camping place. They forgot what had happened when they complained before. They forgot the blessings God had given them. They said, "We are hungry for meat! Remember the good fish we had in Egypt? Remember the melons, the cucumbers and the onions?" The more they whined the hungrier they became.

"We're tired of this manna," they said. "We want meat!" They complained while they gathered manna and whined while they ate it. Finally, like pouting children, they stood in front of their tents and cried because they had no meat. Moses was ashamed of them. He did not feel like praying for them again. Moses told God he was tired of leading these people who acted like children.

God told Moses, "Tell the people they will have meat—not one day or two— but for a whole month. They will have so much meat they will be sick of it." God sent a wind that blew in great flocks of quail. All day and all night and all the next day the people gathered quail.

When they got back to camp they cooked the quail. Then they ate and ate and ate. Many became ill and some died.

**Story from Numbers 11**

34

# Roof Is Torn Up

One day while Jesus was visiting in Capernaum, a crowd of people filled the house until not another person could get in or out. Jesus was preaching and healing the sick. Strange noises started coming from above their heads. Soon the roof began to part and they saw a man on a cot being lowered from the ceiling.

From the roof the crippled man's four friends looked on anxiously. Would Jesus heal their friend? He was not able to move and had to lie on his bed day after day. His friends had tried to bring him to Jesus but could not get through the door because of the crowd. So they took him up on the roof, pulled some tiles back, tied a rope around the sick man's bed and lowered him very carefully into the room right in front of Jesus.

The people in the room wondered what was happening and what Jesus would do. Maybe some of them even knew the sick man. They were surprised when they heard Jesus say, "Son, be of good cheer for your sins are forgiven!" The crowd looked at Jesus in surprise. They knew God could forgive sins but they didn't know he was the Son of God.

Then Jesus said to the man, "Arise, take up your bed and return to your own house." Immediately the man's strength returned. He got up, rolled up his bed and lifted it onto his shoulders. The people were so surprised they made way for him as he walked through the room and into the street to join his happy friends.

**Story from Luke 5:18-20**

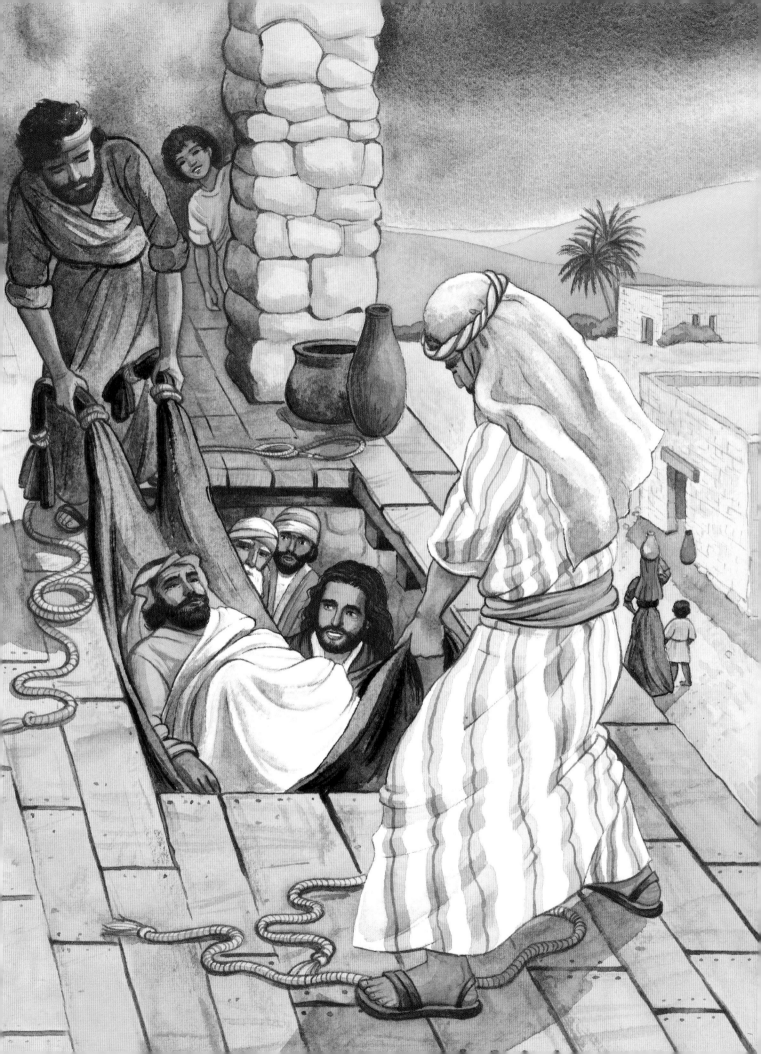

# Samuel Hears God

When Samuel was a small boy his mother and father took him to the high priest, Eli. Samuel's mother said, "I am bringing my little boy to live and to help in the Lord's house."

One night God spoke to Samuel but he did not know it was God. When he heard a voice calling him he thought it was Eli. Quickly Samuel got up out of bed and ran to Eli. "Here I am," he said, and he waited for Eli to say what he wanted. But Eli had not called Samuel and sent him back to bed. The voice called again.

The third time the voice called Eli knew God wanted to speak to the boy. Eli said, "Go and lie down. If the voice calls again, say, 'Speak, Lord, for your servant listens.'"

Samuel ran back to bed and once again the voice called his name. This time he answered, "Speak, Lord, for your servant listens." And God talked with Samuel that night.

Story from 1 Samuel 2:22—3:18

# Ten Commandments

Moses often went to Mount Sinai to talk to God. God told Moses how to lead the people of Israel into the Promised Land. During one trip to speak to God, Moses spent forty days and nights as God gave him rules for the people to follow. Moses wrote them down in a book. But God himself wrote the Ten Commandments on two stone tablets.

## The Ten Commandments

1. Thou shalt have no other gods before me
2. Thou shalt not make unto thee any graven image
3. Thou shalt not take the name of the Lord thy God in vain
4. Remember the Sabbath day to keep it holy
5. Honor thy father and thy mother
6. Thou shalt not kill
7. Thou shalt not commit adultery
8. Thou shalt not steal
9. Thou shalt not bear false witness against thy neighbor
10. Thou shalt not covet

**Story from Exodus 20**

# Upper Room—
## Jesus Shares His Last Supper with the Disciples

When the Passover came Jesus and his disciples met in the upstairs guest room of a friend in Jerusalem. A feeling of sadness crept over them when Jesus said this was his last supper with them. It seemed impossible to the men that anyone ever could kill Jesus. Soon they were talking about other matters at the supper table. Some even wondered who would be the greatest in Jesus' kingdom.

Jesus knew their thoughts and wanted to teach them more about his kingdom. He got up from the table, took off his coat and tied a towel around his waist. Then he began to wash their feet.  The disciples were so surprised. Why would Jesus do this? They had washed their feet before coming into the upper room. They just didn't understand.

When he was finished, Jesus laid aside the towel and put on his coat again. He explained, "You call me Lord, and so I am. If I, your Lord and Master, have washed your feet, you ought to wash one another's feet. The servant is not greater than his master, and if you would be good servants you will obey my words."

After supper Jesus took bread, offered thanks, broke the bread in pieces and gave each disciple a piece. "Take this bread and eat it, for it is my body which is broken for you." Then he took the cup. When he had given thanks he passed it to them saying, "Drink this, for it is my blood, which is shed for you." Jesus knew he was going to die and he wanted to share these last moments with his disciples.

### Story from John 13

# Victory Over Death

After Jesus died his body was placed in a tomb or cave carved out of rock. Very early on Sunday morning the women came to the garden. When they looked inside Jesus' tomb it was empty. What could have happened? They were afraid.

An angel told them, "Do not be afraid. Why are you looking for the living among the dead? Jesus is not here. He is risen as he said. Go quickly and tell his disciples that he is alive."

The women ran from the place, filled with joy. The good news seemed too wonderful to be true. As they ran to tell the disciples and other friends Jesus met them. And the women fell at his feet and worshiped him. Jesus said to them, "Do not be afraid: go tell my friends they should go into Galilee and I will meet them there."

Each Easter we share the joy of his disciples as we remember that Jesus lives.

**Story from Matthew 28:1-10**

# Woman at the Well

One day as Jesus and the disciples were traveling through Samaria Jesus grew very tired. He sat down to rest by a well while his disciples went into the city to buy food.

Soon a woman came to get water at the well. When her jar was full she pulled it up again. Just as she was ready to start back to the city Jesus said, "Give me a drink."

When the woman told Jesus she was surprised he spoke to her he replied, "Whoever drinks the water I give will never be thirsty again." The woman was really interested now but she did not know the living water was Jesus' free gift of salvation.

Jesus told the woman things about herself she thought no one knew. He told her about the wrong things she had done. Leaving her water beside the well, she ran to tell her friends about this wonderful stranger. The people were so curious they went back to Jacob's well with her. Jesus talked with the Samaritans about the things of God. For two days he taught the people and many believed.

**Story from John 4:1-43**

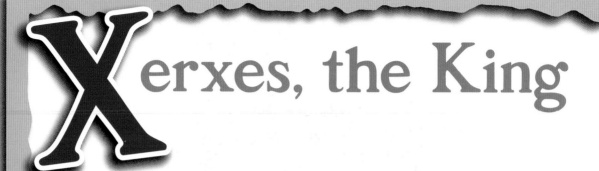

# Xerxes, the King

A Jewish woman named Esther became queen, the wife of King Xerxes. The king and queen loved each other, but he did not know she was Jewish.

Among the princes in the palace of King Xerxes was Haman, a very proud man. He demanded that all the servants bow to him when he passed through the king's gates. All bowed but Mordecai, a Jewish man who was Esther's uncle. Haman was so angry he decided to punish Mordecai and all Jews by having them killed. Haman told the king that the Jews were obeying their own laws instead of the king's. Haman said, "Let a law be made that these people be killed."

Because he trusted Haman the king gave his consent. When Esther heard about the death sentence she went to the king with a request. When he asked her what her request was, she invited the king and Haman to dinner.

At dinner the next day King Xerxes asked, "What is your request, Queen Esther?" When Esther told the king about a plot to kill her and her people, the king was astonished. He asked, "Who is he and where is he who would dare do such a thing?"

"The man is Haman," the queen answered. Haman was more frightened than he had ever been in his life and fell at Esther's feet begging for mercy. The king ordered, "Hang Haman on the gallows he had prepared for Mordecai." Because he loved his wife, King Xerxes saved Queen Esther and all her people from death.

Story from Esther 7-10

# Young Child Made Well

When Jesus entered Galilee news of his coming spread rapidly from one city to another. One man could not wait for Jesus to come to his city. He went looking for Jesus. He was a nobleman, an honored ruler of the city. How worried he was because his little son lay sick with a burning fever! The doctors could not help the little boy.

The nobleman hurried to find Jesus. When he saw Jesus he pleaded with the Master, "Sir, if you do not come at once my son may be dead before we reach him."

Jesus looked kindly at the distressed father. He said, "Go back home. Your son lives." Because the nobleman believed Jesus' words he started back home. He was not afraid for his son any longer—Jesus had said the boy was well.

As the nobleman approached his city his servants ran to meet him. "Your son lives. He is well," they said.

"At what time," asked the nobleman, "did he begin to get better?"

The servants replied, "His fever left him yesterday at the seventh hour." That was the very hour Jesus had told the nobleman that his son would live. The nobleman and his whole household believed in Jesus when they heard how the sick boy had been healed.

**Story from John 4:45-54**

# Zacchaeus Meets Jesus

Jesus and his friends were walking down the streets of Jericho. When they came to a large tree Jesus stopped. He looked up and called, "Zacchaeus, come down."

A man came sliding down the tree trunk. This was Zacchaeus, a very rich man. He had never seen Jesus before but had heard many things about him. When news came to the city that Jesus was coming, short Zacchaeus had climbed the tree to see him.

Jesus knew all about Zacchaeus. He knew how rich he was. He knew too that Zacchaeus had cheated many people.

Zacchaeus was surprised to hear Jesus say, "I am going to visit your house today."

After talking with Jesus, Zacchaeus was sorry for his sins. He asked Jesus to forgive him. Jesus brought peace and joy to Zacchaeus.

**Story from Luke 19:2-10**

# Alphabet for Boys and Girls A-M

**A**ct kindly

**B**e honest

**C**are about others

**D**o your best

**E**njoy God's world

**F**orgive quickly

**G**o happily to church

**H**ave time to learn well

**I**nvite others to church

**J**oin in family worship

**K**eep trying

**L**ove God with all your heart

**M**ake many friends

# Alphabet for Boys and Girls

## N-Z

**N**otice ways to be thankful

**O**bey your parents

**P**ray often

**Q**uit doing anything that is wrong

**R**ead the Bible

**S**hare what you have

**T**ell the truth

**U**se your time well

**V**isit the old and the sick

**W**ork hard but with joy

E**X**cel in doing good

**Y**ield (give) yourself to God

Be **Z**ealous for what is right